Social Skills for the Everyday Person

Luzard Christopher Henry

Copyright © 2019 Luzard Christopher Henry
All rights reserved.

Book layout by ebooklaunch.com

Introduction

Hello, my name is Luzard Christopher Henry. I am a 24 year old, young Black male, from the tri-cities area of Virginia. I graduated high school in June 2013, from Prince George High School, in Prince George County Virginia. I continued my education at the illustrious Norfolk State University, in Norfolk, Virginia, choosing Business Management as my major. With a lot of determination and perseverance, I graduated in the fall of 2017. I am currently working full time for Ocean Network Express doing documentation of bills and customer service.

I have experienced a few things in my early stage of adulthood. Therefore, my reason for writing this book, is to use my life experiences (up to this point) to reach out and assist those in the age range of 18-26. However, anyone is welcome to read this book, be it out of curiosity or to pick up some pointers. I find it fascinating that the young adults today are very anti-social and more into social media. It is my purpose and desire to give a young adult's point of view on how social skills could be developed

CONTENTS

Introduction	i
1. Introducing yourself	1
2. Networking	5
3. Keeping in Touch	11
4. Promoting Yourself	15
5. Showing Affection	19
Conclusion	23
References	25

CHAPTER 1

INTRODUCING YOURSELF

WHETHER IT IS IN A school setting, a social event, or a job interview, introducing yourself is perhaps the most important step when it comes to socializing. Personally, I feel as if young people today do not really know how to make a good impression. For example, there are so many outside influences on people, to the point where they feel like they have to be something they are not, just to fit in or make friends. The greatest approach is to be yourself and show people the genuine you. However, depending on the environment in which you find yourself, you may have to make an adjustment on how you want to approach someone or a group of people. For instance if you are at a party, it is a lot easier to introduce yourself and be you, because there will not be so much attention on you if everyone around you are enjoying themselves, so it is not difficult to make conversation or hold a person's attention. Whereas, in a school setting or public setting, you need to have a friendly or approachable demeanor. Remember, everyone was not raised or brought up the same as you, so you cannot assume your usual way of communicating is fine. Of course, be yourself, but still be respectful to everyone and you should receive the same reaction back. It is a common practice to show respect in order to receive respect. Whether it is from a millionaire, or even someone who is homeless, show respect.

Another key point in a new interaction is body language. This could also be the same as demeanor, but a little more critical. When talking with someone, make eye contact, stand tall, and relax. It is very common to feel nervous when talking to someone new, but you do not have to show it. People often show signs of interest in body language more than they do the person who is actually talking. So, with that being said, check your body language when talking to people. It is not hard to pick up on these things regardless if you are looking for them or not. If a person is looking off into space or in their phone, or just clearly not paying attention, they most likely are not into the engagement. Another reason could be they have bad social skills. Who knows. But from a general stand point, please show interest in first interactions and you will see positive results in more social interactions to come. Once body language and demeanor become easier for you to control, you will find yourself becoming more of an approachable person.

Another key point to introducing yourself, is holding an actual conversation. This can be a bit challenging if you have not already picked a reason in your head to talk to someone. Again, this plays into your environment you are in. I find it easier to already have a reason or topic when I approach someone.

School is the best place for sparking these conversations, which is why I chose the audience of 18-26. That is the common age for most people to be in high school or college; therefore you are around your peers who most likely are your age. But for my readers who may be a bit older, you still probably work with people who are close to your age. Back to the topic at hand; when holding a conversation, be interesting or at least have a good reason for speaking. If someone approached you and gave you horrible conversation you would be quite upset for having your time wasted. With that being said, have everything planned out in your head and go for it, with whomever or whatever it is that you are trying to accomplish. I think the easiest method is, asking a question of common interest. Here are some common examples: "Hey, did you do the homework?", "Whose music do you like to listen to?", or "Do you know any good places to hang out at?". There are other ways to come up with your own style of starting a conversation, but those are basic examples for getting through the nervous stage of approaching someone. The one unknown variable, is how long to hold a conversation. "Should I talk for 5 or 50 minutes?", that is the fun part about being social, you never know what someone could be thinking or know what someone might have to offer. If you want to know the actual duration of a conversation, it is 3 minutes and 5 seconds for guys and 3 minutes and 20 seconds for women (*Mixed-Gender Conversations vs Real Space*). Makes sense to me, because guys usually want to get straight to the point, while women are more thoughtful. Then again, that is me generally speaking. Everyone is different. It can be the opposite sometimes.

Another key point of socializing is speaking in groups. This is an extremely underrated tactic to me. If you are talking to a group of people for the first time, it is best to speak on topics you know. Nobody wants to hear about basketball if the subject is football or nobody wants to talk about going natural if the conversation is on sew-ins. Even if you speak once or several times, mental notes are taken by your peers on what you are saying. If you are more knowledgeable on a certain topic, people will associate you with that topic with the next social interaction. Talking in small groups can also be a good way to build confidence, while working on talking in front of larger groups of people.

With the conclusion of this chapter, I hope I have given some tips on how to first start off with social skills and maybe even eliminate social anxiety. I am not an expert, but I have, through my 24 years of living, come across great ways to communicate and socialize better with people, using what I have told you in this chapter.

CHAPTER 2

NETWORKING

NETWORKING TODAY IS PROBABLY one of the most powerful tools a person can have, especially if used correctly. Now, depending on how much you actually use a social media cite or app, this chapter might not even matter to you, but it will still be useful information. Social media can be applied in many different ways, but it varies with each individual's desire. With that being said, I will divide this chapter into three categories, representing three types of people.

Category 1 is a person who uses social media just for the purpose of being social; a social butterfly. If that is the case with you, you probably do not even need to read this book and maybe just bought this to support me. I appreciate you, but anyways, people who use social media for social purposes can be very powerful if they go about things correctly. Going back to chapter 1, with introducing yourself and holding a conversation; that is the perfect time to throw your social media account in the conversation; that is, if they have not asked or mentioned it. If you are a category 1 person, you are most likely popular, so social media is like a tool to you more than it is something to waste time. If you have a large following, you know about the most hip events, who you should and should not talk to, and lastly rumors. Now of course with social media being a powerful tool, you should use it accordingly; meaning, it is better to show yourself more positively than negatively. People will make judgements about you off these sites and apps, before you even talk to them. Therefore my advice to you is show people what you want, but make sure it is something good. Like I just mentioned, "rumors" are very common when it comes to using social media as a means of popularity. No one wants a bad name for themselves over social media that can affect your professional career and may lead to other negative things to occur. Another benefit for the category 1 person is knowing all the best events or best spots. People who have a large following get notified or "hit up" about the most popular events. Since I am speaking to the young adults, that could mean parties, food spots, what games to attend, concerts, and many other things. It all depends on you; that is the fun part about making social media useful for yourself. If you are indeed a category 1 person, please keep things positive and use social media to its maximum potential.

Secondly, there is category 2. Category 2 is a person who uses social media for personal reasons. Some examples would be, keeping up with family members, photography, blogging, posting food, and maybe informing people about a specific topic. You may not be interested in having a large following, but it is still important to network yourself when meeting people. Get your message out there for people to know who and what you stand for. As far as keeping in touch with family members, I think social media is a great way to keep in contact with people who may live far from you. This could lead to road trips or setting up a family event in the future. Like I said for the category 1 person, please be mindful of your content. Social media does not have an age requirement, so your young family members or close friends can get access to what you post sometimes. Keep things positive and please keep in contact with people. That one unexpected text or call can go a long way for some people. Just to know someone out there thought about you today, means a lot. For those of you who just post your interests or experiences, it is beneficial to have a large following, but not priority. Personally, the category 2 people are those who like to vacation, cook, draw, model, share poetry, music and etc. So depending on how passionate you are with your craft or stuff you post will show how much you care about what you are doing. It is important to have great content with what you are posting for your following. Be honest. No one wants to keep track of bland images or text. If it is clear that you do not care or put forth any effort with what you post, the numbers will tell it all. So with that being said, your content could mean 100 followers or 100,000 followers. The choice is always yours. If you know your posts are not very popular topics or may offend people, I suggest you keep things private and only network with people who are similar to you. Like I said before, social media is very powerful, so use it wisely.

Lastly, the category 3 person is someone who uses social media for business purposes. These people usually have more than one account on many different platforms. It makes sense for category 3 people to always mention their accounts when socializing. This is one of your forms of income, potential customers. Social media and income are limitless if you find the right niche. I would recommend having a large following if you are the category 3 person. Regardless of what your product is, it is best to post positive and good reviews. If you are not meeting standards, people in today's world are not afraid to let you know if you are putting out bad products. Another way networking can be useful is finding out what people like and do not like. Before you launch a product or service, you can conduct surveys and take down people's thoughts on whatever it is you are trying to sell. I think the category 3 person has the most potential when it comes to networking. Why do I think that? When it comes to passion and drive, it really shows when it comes to networking. Just let the numbers speak for themselves. Your success will only show with your numbers. Which is why I think the category 3 person should network a lot and make social media one of their most useful tools. As stated with the previous categories, please show yourself to be positive. Be professional of course and about your business, because people like to have a comforting feeling when it comes to investing in a product or service. Please keep that in mind when networking for yourself or others. Nobody wants a bad name when it comes to making a profit or holding a business name.

It is extremely important to keep a good image. Whether your name holds weight on campus, at work, or in life in general, always let your name come with positive and influential things.

With each one of these categories, it is a smart move to keep in contact with your following, which can vary depending on the size, but the effort never goes unnoticed. No matter which category you fit, there are good benefits from each. I think networking plays deeply into opportunity. There is a very common saying; "It is not always about what you know, but who you know". I think I said that right, but you get what I am saying. There are endless possibilities from each person you come across in life. I am not saying to use people, but find something positive from each person you decide to network or socialize with. Everybody has something to offer no matter what aspect of life they are in, or what you are in. With that being said, always be the same you, with each interaction. You really do not want to hear things about yourself that is not true. You get more respect being yourself, than being something you are not, just to be popular. So, once you become fluent and confident in networking and socializing, you can expand whatever you have to offer a lot easier. Use these tips and insight and I promise you will find yourself doing a whole lot more with your free time.

Chapter 3

Keeping in Touch

THERE IS ONE THING THAT I have learned in my life, and that is, check on people. I do not mean to be morbid, but you just never know when you will live your last day. No matter who you are or what you do, it is always appreciated when someone checks on you. A call, text, or even a post on a social media page—it all counts.I think people are too temporary these days. My opinion on that is, be upfront with your intentions; that goes back to the first 2 chapters. Let people know your reason for speaking, because no one likes their valuable time to be wasted. Consequently, the effort with keeping in touch varies as always with you. I have found four points that I think will help those of you, who may not have an idea on what it is you should do to keep in touch.

My first point is, call people. I know we live in an age where technology makes interactions a lot easier behind a screen, but calling is still effective. Nothing beats face to face interaction, FYI. When you decide to call someone make sure you have your thoughts together before calling the person. Awkward silence is a conversation killer. Even if it is with a friend or family member, it still sucks to be silent on the phone. The usual main reasons for keeping in touch is, checking on the person, asking what they have planned for themselves, ask them what events they may have planned, and if they are in school, ask them how school is going. I will warn you, depending on how hard life has been on a person, you may run into a case, so be prepared for an hour long conversation from that one person. Another call could be checking on an old mentor; that could be a coach, teacher, or manager. It is essential to keep mentors around, sometimes you may run into a tough spot in life and need advice; sometimes parents and family members might not always have the best insight, so ask a mentor— just some side advice. Also, keeping in touch with mentors can affect your job hunt. I think references are pretty big when it comes to jobs, so that is where keeping in touch with mentors come along. Keeping professional contacts goes a long way, especially if you are in a rough patch and might need some assistance.

 I feel it is also important to keep in touch with old friends, maybe from your younger days; such as middle school or elementary. If you are still in high school or are fairly young, you probably do this anyway. Keeping in touch with old friends can really have a positive effect. Going over old stories, talking about old crushes and discussing how things used to be can give you a humbling feeling. Just to go over how far you have come, to me, shows growth. Another reason to keep in touch with old friends is traveling. That might be the most beneficial thing about keeping in touch—planning trips while catching up. Once you get to college or start your career, you often meet people from different places. This all falls under being social. So that one random conversation could turn into a trip to anywhere, you never know until you try.

For those of you who keep in touch for business purposes, you know it is important to always keep a line of communication for customers or business relationships. With each new social interaction, there could come income or opportunity. Just think of how much better you would feel after spending money and the store or service called you a few weeks later and asked, "How was the product was and how could we improve it?" A small gesture, but it shows concern. Anyone who has worked with customer service knows that keeping in touch goes a long way.

Keeping in touch for the dating aspect, may get a little sketchy. That varies for you personally. Speaking from experience, I would never deny communication from a past interest or love. It all depends on how things ended. If it was a genuine relationship, keeping in touch is never a problem. You still have to respect boundaries. The positive aspect from this could be that old issues are resolved peacefully as friends. The two of you could have a better understanding of each other, and lastly, between you two, there could be something better. I am not going to go into too much detail with dating, but staying positive with everything and keeping your mind towards growing will never fail you.

Overall, a small act of caring can turn into much more. Even if it is for a few minutes, you still showed enough care to actually think about someone else. You made the choice to actually expand your social circle and open up new pathways for yourself and others. I think keeping in touch goes a long way for every person, no matter where they are in life. Lastly, please use this chapter in your daily or monthly routine. I promise, someone will thank you every time you decide to check on them.

Chapter 4

Promoting Yourself

Promoting yourself sounds pretty simple, but it is actually a very complex and difficult thing to do when you sit down and analyze yourself. You might sit down and think, what is it that I actually like about myself? What things should people know about me? People look at celebrities, musicians, and popular people and sit back and wonder, "How did they become that?" I am certain that they all started with themselves and eventually just grew on the world. One thing I have noticed is, you will only go as far as YOU allow yourself to go. There will always be opposition and doubt, which is a part of life; but how we respond is what makes life even better. There is nothing you cannot do if you just have faith or belief in yourself.

Share your goals, when you are promoting yourself, because people want to know what you have planned for the future. Where do you planto be in 5 or 10 years from now? Be confident about your goals, no matter how big or small they are. Again, you, the individual, are special and anything you decide to pursue should be known when it comes to promoting yourself and your goals. Nobody wants to hear boring stuff, so be specific and detailed about your goals and where you want to be. Be honest. Do you really listen when you hear regular stuff? People want to hear or see vivid pictures being painted in their mind about what you will accomplish. I have an old college roommate, who always talked about being wealthy and graduating early, so that he can get a head start in his field. In college you always hear goals from people. The common goal is to graduate; but I can honestly say, I watched my roommate stay up and take trips to the library almost every week, turning down parties or any chance to turn up. He made small sacrifices for a bigger reward. He was a computer science major. If you are in college, you know how difficult that major is. My past roommate was a pretty confident guy, so everything lined up for the most part. He eventually graduated May 2017 and then graduated from grad school December 2018, all while still being 23 years of age. My past roommate really went out and accomplished his goals. You really can accomplish anything, even while being young. It just takes focus; especially when it comes to your goals.

    Another part of promoting yourself is giving off good energy. Energy is the truest part of a person. No matter how you act, your energy will always attract itself. What you are putting out there will come back to you. For example, if you are trying to make money, you will most likely gravitate to those who are doing the same thing. Yeah, it might suck to cut off longtime friends, but in order to progress and go toward your goals in life, you must assemble the right people to do that. Being positive also keeps your image and respect unblemished. If your peers always view you as a peaceful and nice person, no rumor or bad news can affect you.

Reliability, to me, is also a vital part of promoting yourself. Let's be honest. Who does not love a person who is always there or always does what they say? I love people who keep their word. Even if it's just a small favor. I promise you, 9 out of 10 times, people will come to you for everything if you are a reliable person. Yeah it gets tough sometimes always being the go to person; at the end of the day though, it pays off. The more you do for others, the more people will do for you. The golden rule, treat others the way you want to be treated. So, if you are reliable you should expect the same thing from others, and if they cannot do that, you have the right to cut them off, whether its family members or friends. This applies to everyone.

Confidence is another key point to promoting yourself. Having confidence carries you in any part of life. Whether its sports, dating, jobs, or just speaking to people. Even if you are not confident, act like it, because no one will really know except you. Confidence only attracts confident people. There is a very thin line between confidence and being cocky. You see, a cocky person really just full of themselves. They might not even have anything great to look back on that they have done. Cocky people really just talk a good game and never have too much to show for it. A confident person has proof to back up his/her talk. A confident person will not just talk about it, but will be about it. If people have a problem with you being confident, they obviously have something they need to work on themselves. Belittling yourself is not okay and it never will be. I would never take someone serious if they always point out their flaws. No one is perfect and we all have issues, but you do not have to announce that. People will only see what you allow them to. Social media has plenty of examples of people who are not the most attractive or the most athletic, yet they portray confidence and people love it. Confidence also rubs off on people. If you look at all the great leaders of today, like Barack Obama, he portrays a confident demeanor. Even after the presidency he still has power and influence. No matter what life throws at you, if you apply yourself confidently, you will overcome anything.

Chapter 5

Showing Affection

I CAN IMAGINE THE LOOK on most people's face when they see the title of this chapter. You are probably pondering on this. What does affection have to do with being social? Well if you ever look at any normal societies outside of America, most countries are pretty heavy with touch or affection as a normal thing. Not just for lovers or family, but with friends and acquaintances. Non-verbal interactions speak louder than words in some instances. For example, instead of discussing a disagreement, some people would rather fight or, instead of telling someone how much you like them, you could kiss them instead. Whether negative or positive, non-verbal communication is impactful.

I think it is very common now for people to not show affection. It might not even be the person's fault; this could be from a person's childhood. Let us look at babies for example. Babies cannot talk, but they can make noise and show movements. Something non-verbal a baby might enjoy is a hug or kiss from a family member or parent, and you do not need words to see if the baby enjoys the interaction with you. If a baby is not happy with you, they will most likely cry or pull away from you. Non-verbal communication is very simple and can be communicated clearly even by babies.

How can you add non-verbal affection into your social interactions? First, start with simple gestures like handshakes or hugs. I think handshakes are the number one universal non-verbal interaction. Even if you just follow the person on social media, if there is a common interest or mutual friend you still give a handshake or as most people call it, "dap up". With that simple gesture, just about anything could happen. You could start a conversation with the person, find out information on something or just keep it moving. Literally, something so small and basic could turn into anything.

Hugs on the other hand, are a little more personal. Hugs are also common, but most likely a friendship is already established. I am going to add some personal feedback on hugs. Do not give someone a one arm hug. The only exception for a one arm hug, is if you are hugging like a group of people. Other than that, have a heart, because a person can tell if you really wanted to hug them or not. People can tell when something is genuine, which is why in the previous chapters I mentioned to always be genuine. Hugging and handshakes are not that deep, but at the same time, they do go a long way, even for first impressions.

Secondly, affection is more effective for the lines of dating or family interactions. I am pretty sure, most of us can agree, when you hurt yourself as a child, your mother's or father's touch, made you feel better. There was no medicine involved, but genuine love and touch is all it takes sometimes. Affection can really take things to another level. Even if you have gone the majority of your life not showing affection, it is never too late to add it to your life. As long as you are genuine and give off good energy, people will enjoy it. When it comes to dating, can you really be into someone that does not show affection? No matter how good a person looks or how much money you might have, a person still needs to feel your love for them. This goes for families too. From birth to adulthood, a person needs affection. This not only affects them, but even the people they deal with. So if you are one of those people who are not affectionate, please incorporate it into your life. This small change will be effective for you and everyone else you deal with. I would actually like to make a reference to Maslow's hierarchy of needs. Human contact is actually one out of the five needs we need socially to gain another step to self-actualization. Self-actualization is when you have met your full potential, so why not hone in on social needs in your life (Web.stanford.edu, 2019).

Lastly, non-verbal affection can affect the business world also. What does touch have to do with money? Why do I need to show affection to someone to gain a profit? These questions probably have not crossed your mind, but involving non-verbal communication does change a person's feeling about spending money or supporting a cause. I would support someone who gives me a handshake or hug, before I put money in the pocket of a person who does not care to interact with me. A more common example of a non-verbal form of affection would be the first handshake with a business partner. Depending on how firm or how soft a handshake is, it can show a lot within those few seconds. If a person has a firm handshake, the other person is more likely to think that they are assertive. Whereas, a soft handshake could show a person as passive. That judgement alone can affect how much money you and you potential business partner plan on making. If you have a business and you want people to support you, hug them or give a handshake after a sell. It is a small gesture, but you just gave your customer a good feeling after spending money. So now when they think about your product, they will think about the caring feeling you gave them. So yes, money and touch have something to do with each other.

Affection/non-verbal communication goes such a long way with people. Some things are practiced and others are natural, which solely depends on you as a person. If you decide to improve on these things, I promise it will work out for the better. I believe that out of everything that I have written about in this short book, this is one of the most important things I hope you learn, because it affects everyone. Your intent while doing it will immediately be received, whether negative or positive, it will affect a person.

Conclusion

WHILE SOCIAL SKILLS SEEMS to be a fleeting thing amongst this generation, I believe that there is still hope. There is a wealth of information that you could search on the internet. However, I just ask that you practice all of the insight that I have given you; practice does make perfect. Small starts never go unnoticed. Even if you are starting off talking to one person, that is a step in the right direction. Social skills can come naturally for some people, but for those who experience anxiety, I hope this book gives you a new outlook.

Most people today believe that they can get things done alone, thinking, "Why should I talk to people, I work better alone." This could be true, but if you look at any successful person, you will notice, they always have a team. One person might be the face, but everyone has a role. To get to that point, you have to expand your social circle. Everyone is not your friend, but if you keep your intent clear and make it obvious why you are speaking to a person, you will see fake relationships dissolve out of your life.

No matter what, please be genuine and true to whatever it is that you are doing. Whether it is working with people, communicating on social media, doing an interview, giving a speech, or even having a phone conversation, people deserve to feel your real emotion. Regardless of what aspect in life the people or person you are dealing with is in, if you keep it honest with them, they will do the same. So, with that being said, go talk to someone. Keep your intentions clear, be confident, and thrive socially. Everything that you have ever wanted could spark from a conversation. I am not a social guru or the most popular person, however, I am an everyday person, writing to my everyday people.

References

Web.stanford.edu. (2019). *Mixed-Gender Conversations vs Real Space*. [online] Available at: https://web.stanford.edu/class/pwr3-25/group2/projects/chris/chris-3.html [Accessed 24 Feb. 2019].

Web.stanford.edu. (2019). *Mixed-Gender Conversations vs Real Space*. [online] Available at: https://web.stanford.edu/class/pwr3-25/group2/projects/chris/chris-3.html [Accessed 10 Mar. 2019].

www.ingramcontent.com/pod-product-compliance
Lightning Source LLC
Chambersburg PA
CBHW021854170526
45157CB00006B/2449